MEDITATION FOR BEGINNERS

2025

An Easy Guide to Finding Calm and Focus

Alex C. Wei

Copyright © 2024 Alex C. Wei.

All rights reserved. No part of this publication may be reproduced, distributed, or transmitted in any form or by any means, including photocopying, recording, or other electronic or mechanical methods, without the prior written permission of the publisher, except in the case of brief quotations embodied in critical reviews and certain other noncommercial uses permitted by copyright law.

Legal Notice:

This book is copyright-protected. It is only for personal use. You cannot amend, distribute, sell, use, quote, or paraphrase any part of the content within this book without the consent of the author or publisher.

Disclaimer Notice:

Please note the information contained within this document is for educational and entertainment purposes only. All efforts have been executed to present accurate, up-to-date, reliable, and complete information. No warranties of any kind are declared or implied. Readers acknowledge that the author is not engaged in the rendering of legal, financial, medical, or professional advice. The content within this book has been derived from various sources. Please consult a licensed professional before attempting any techniques outlined in this book.

By reading this document, the reader agrees that under no circumstances is the author responsible for any losses, direct or indirect, that are incurred as a result of the use of the information contained within this document, including, but not limited to, errors, omissions, or inaccuracies.

Dedication

This book is dedicated to those who seek calm and focus in a chaotic world. May you find calmness through the simple yet transformative practice of meditation.

Content

Introduction

In a world that often feels chaotic and overwhelming, finding moments of calm and focus has never been more essential. ***Meditation for Beginners 2025: An Easy Guide to Finding Calm and Focus*** is designed to help you embark on your journey into meditation, a practice rooted in ancient traditions that has gained significant recognition for its mental and physical health benefits.

Whether you're seeking to reduce stress, improve your concentration, or simply create a sense of inner peace, this book will guide you step by step. We'll explore the fundamentals of meditation, the science behind its effectiveness, and practical techniques tailored for beginners. You'll discover how just a few minutes of meditation each day can lead to profound changes in your overall well-being.

This guide isn't just about learning how to meditate; it's about integrating mindfulness into your daily life, fostering resilience against stress, and cultivating a deeper connection with yourself. As you turn these pages, you'll find that meditation can be simple, accessible, and transformative. Let's begin this journey together and unlock the calm and focus that awaits within you.

Chapter 1: Understanding Meditation

Meditation is a practice that transcends cultures and time, offering a pathway to inner peace and heightened awareness. At its core, meditation involves training the mind to focus and redirect thoughts, promoting a deeper understanding of oneself and one's surroundings.

Definition of Meditation

Meditation can be defined as a set of techniques that encourage an enhanced state of awareness and focused attention. It is often employed to achieve mental clarity, emotional stability, and spiritual growth. While there are various forms of meditation—such as mindfulness, transcendental meditation, and guided meditation—the common thread among them is the intention to cultivate a calm and focused mind.

Different Types of Meditation

1. **Mindfulness Meditation**: This practice involves paying attention to the present moment without judgment. Practitioners often focus on their breath or bodily sensations, observing thoughts and feelings as they arise and pass away. Mindfulness meditation has been shown to reduce anxiety and improve emotional regulation.

2. **Transcendental Meditation (TM)**: TM is a specific form of silent mantra meditation developed by Maharishi Mahesh Yogi. It involves the repetition of a specific sound or phrase, allowing practitioners to transcend ordinary thought and experience a state of deep rest and tranquility.

3. **Guided Meditation**: In guided meditation, a narrator or teacher provides instructions, often leading listeners through visualization exercises

or relaxation techniques. This form can be particularly beneficial for beginners, as it offers structure and direction.

4. **Loving-Kindness Meditation (Metta)**: This technique focuses on developing an attitude of love and compassion towards oneself and others. Practitioners repeat phrases that express goodwill and kindness, promoting feelings of empathy and connection .

Historical Background and Cultural Significance

Meditation has roots in ancient traditions, with evidence of its practice found in the earliest texts of Hinduism, Buddhism, and Taoism. In Eastern philosophies, meditation has long been regarded as a means to attain spiritual enlightenment and personal transformation. Over the past few decades, Western cultures have embraced meditation as a tool for stress management and mental health improvement, leading to a growing body of research supporting its effectiveness .

Understanding the basics of meditation sets the foundation for a meaningful practice. In the following chapters, we will explore the science behind meditation, practical techniques for beginners, and how to create a consistent meditation routine that fits seamlessly into your life. By embracing this journey, you will unlock the potential for greater calm and focus, transforming not just your mind, but your entire experience of life.

Chapter 2: The Science Behind Meditation

Meditation is not just an ancient practice; it's also supported by modern science as an effective way to enhance mental and physical well-being. In this chapter, we will explore the scientific research that highlights the benefits of meditation, how it affects the brain, and its impact on overall health.

Overview of Scientific Research

Numerous studies have shown that meditation can lead to significant improvements in mental health. Research indicates that regular meditation practice can reduce stress, anxiety, and depression while increasing overall emotional well-being. For instance, a meta-analysis published in *Psychological Bulletin* found that mindfulness meditation significantly reduces symptoms of anxiety and depression, making it a valuable tool for mental health .

Benefits for Mental Health

1. **Stress Reduction**: Meditation activates the body's relaxation response, lowering cortisol levels, which are linked to stress. Research from Harvard University demonstrated that mindfulness meditation can decrease stress by enhancing emotional regulation .

2. **Improved Focus and Attention**: Studies have shown that meditation can improve attention span and concentration. A study in the journal *Cognition* found that just two weeks of mindfulness training can enhance focus and cognitive flexibility .

3. **Emotional Regulation**: Regular meditation practice helps individuals manage their emotions more effectively. Neuroimaging studies have shown that meditation can lead to structural changes in brain regions associated with emotional regulation, such as the prefrontal cortex .

Physical Health Benefits

1. **Lower Blood Pressure**: Meditation has been linked to lower blood pressure, which can reduce the risk of heart disease. Research published in *Circulation: Cardiovascular Quality and Outcomes* found that mindfulness practices significantly lower blood pressure in individuals with hypertension .

2. **Enhanced Immune Function**: Some studies suggest that meditation can boost the immune system. Research in the journal *Psychosomatic Medicine* found that participants who practiced meditation had higher levels of immune response compared to those who did not .

The science behind meditation provides compelling evidence for its effectiveness as a tool for enhancing mental and physical health. By understanding these benefits, you are better equipped to appreciate the value of incorporating meditation into your daily routine. In the following chapters, we will delve into practical techniques that you can use to start your meditation practice and make it a part of your lifestyle.

Chapter 3: Getting Started with Meditation

Embarking on your meditation journey can be both exciting and a bit daunting. In this chapter, we will cover how to prepare for meditation, find the right environment, and set achievable goals that will help you establish a consistent practice.

Preparing for Meditation

Before you begin, it's important to create the right mindset and environment. *Here are some steps to help you get started:*

1. **Choose a Quiet Space**: Find a place where you can sit comfortably without distractions. This could be a quiet room in your home, a park, or any space where you feel at ease.
2. **Set a Regular Time**: Consistency is key in building a meditation habit. Choose a specific

time each day to practice, whether it's morning, afternoon, or evening.

3. **Wear Comfortable Clothing**: Dress in loose, comfortable clothing that allows you to sit or lie down without restriction.

Basic Meditation Postures and Techniques

1. **Seated Posture**: Sit on a chair or cushion with your back straight but relaxed. Place your hands on your knees or in your lap.
2. **Lying Down**: If sitting is uncomfortable, you can lie down on your back, keeping your arms at your sides.
3. **Mindful Breathing**: Focus on your breath as you inhale and exhale. Notice the sensations of the air entering and leaving your body.

Setting Realistic Goals for Your Practice

Start small to avoid feeling overwhelmed. Aim for just 5 to 10 minutes of meditation daily, gradually increasing the duration as you become more comfortable. Remember, it's not about perfection; it's about consistency and progress.

Chapter 4: Simple Meditation Techniques for Beginners

Now that you are prepared to meditate, let's explore some simple techniques that are perfect for beginners. These methods will help you develop your practice and find what resonates best with you.

Step-by-Step Instructions for Basic Meditation Practices

1. **Breathing Meditation**:
   - Sit comfortably and close your eyes.
   - Inhale deeply through your nose, counting to four.
   - Hold your breath for a moment, then exhale slowly through your mouth, counting to six.
   - Focus on your breath, gently bringing your attention back whenever your mind wanders.

2. **Body Scan**:

    o   Lie down comfortably with your eyes closed.

    o   Take a few deep breaths, then bring your awareness to your toes.

    o   Gradually move your attention up through your body, noticing any sensations or tension.

    o   Relax each area as you focus on it, releasing any tension you find.

3. **Guided Visualization**:

    o   Find a comfortable position and close your eyes.

    o   Imagine a peaceful place, such as a beach or forest.

    o   Engage your senses—what do you see, hear, and smell?

    o   Allow yourself to relax in this tranquil setting for a few minutes.

Tips for Overcoming Common Challenges

- **Distractions**: If your mind wanders, gently acknowledge the thought and bring your focus back to your breath or body.
- **Restlessness**: If you feel restless, try a different posture or change the duration of your session.

Chapter 5: Creating a Consistent Meditation Practice

Establishing a consistent meditation routine is crucial for experiencing its full benefits. In this chapter, we'll discuss strategies to help you make meditation a regular part of your life.

Importance of Consistency

Meditation is most effective when practiced regularly. Aim to meditate daily, even if for just a few minutes. This consistency will deepen your practice and enhance its benefits.

Strategies for Building a Daily Practice

1. **Set Reminders**: Use your phone or a calendar to set daily reminders for your meditation time.

2. **Join a Group**: Consider joining a local meditation group or participating in online sessions. The community can provide motivation and support.

3. **Track Your Progress**: Keep a meditation journal to record your thoughts, feelings, and experiences. Reflecting on your journey can encourage you to continue.

Utilizing Meditation Apps and Resources

There are numerous meditation apps available that provide guided meditations, timers, and progress tracking. Popular apps include:

- **Headspace**
- **Calm**
- **Insight Timer**

These resources can help you stay motivated and explore new techniques.

Chapter 6: Enhancing Your Meditation Experience

As you become more comfortable with meditation, you may want to explore ways to enhance your practice. This chapter will provide tips on incorporating mindfulness into your daily life and using additional resources to deepen your experience.

Incorporating Mindfulness into Daily Activities

Mindfulness can be practiced outside of meditation sessions. Here are some ways to integrate mindfulness into your daily routine:

1. **Mindful Eating**: Pay attention to the taste, texture, and aroma of your food. Eat slowly and savor each bite.

2. **Mindful Walking**: During a walk, focus on the sensations of your feet touching the ground, the

rhythm of your breath, and the sights and sounds around you.

3. **Mindful Listening**: When conversing with someone, give them your full attention. Listen without planning your response, and truly engage in the moment.

Using Music, Guided Meditations, or Nature Sounds

Incorporating soothing music or nature sounds into your practice can enhance relaxation. Many guided meditation apps offer soundscapes to create a calming environment. Experiment with different sounds to find what resonates with you.

Journaling and Reflecting on Your Meditation Journey

Keeping a meditation journal can help you track your progress and insights. After each session, jot down any thoughts, feelings, or experiences. Reflecting on your journey can deepen your understanding and commitment to the practice.

By developing a consistent meditation practice and incorporating mindfulness into your daily life, you can experience the profound benefits of meditation. As you continue your journey, remember that meditation is a personal experience—there's no right or wrong way to do it. Embrace your unique path, and allow the calm and focus of meditation to enrich your life.

Conclusion

Congratulations on taking the first steps toward a fulfilling meditation practice! As you have explored in this book, meditation is not just a technique; it's a pathway to greater calm, focus, and overall well-being.

Throughout our journey, we've uncovered the science behind meditation, discovered simple techniques tailored for beginners, and established strategies for creating a consistent practice. By incorporating mindfulness into your daily activities and utilizing resources like meditation apps, you can enrich your experience and maintain your commitment to personal growth.

Remember, meditation is a personal journey—there is no one-size-fits-all approach. Allow yourself the freedom to explore various techniques and find what resonates most with you. The benefits of meditation, from reduced stress and improved focus to enhanced emotional regulation, can profoundly impact your life.

As you move forward, keep your practice flexible and adaptable. Celebrate your progress, however small, and be patient with yourself as you navigate the ups and downs of this transformative journey. Embrace the moments of stillness and clarity, and watch as they ripple into every aspect of your life.

Thank you for choosing this book as your guide. May your meditation practice bring you peace, focus, and joy for years to come!

www.ingramcontent.com/pod-product-compliance
Lightning Source LLC
Chambersburg PA
CBHW051724250726

48653CB00008B/3184